teeth of the world

ashley capes

teeth of the world

Copyright Ashley Capes ©2019

Cover Art: Erik Ly
Layout & Typset: Close-Up Books

All rights reserved. No part of this book may be reproduced in any form by any electronic or mechanical means including photocopying, recording, or information storage and retrieval without permission in writing from the authors.

ISBN-978-0-6483957-2-0

Published by Close-Up Books
Melbourne, Australia

For Brooke

acknowledgements

Many of the poems in this collection first appeared at www.ashleycapes.com but additional pieces also appeared at:

seashores, haiku hub, failed haiku, the heron's nest and *medium.*

Thanks to the editors of the above publications for their support.

I would also like to thank my loved ones, as ever, for making each day worthwhile.

First

no more red leaves
raincoats
fill the street

flood water –
my neighbour's house
on tiptoes

clearing undergrowth
in winter
trash desaturated

and there's the moon
a pale shadow of bone
this morning

foggy morning –
hovering
between memories

waiting
for the next train
you are my coat

open fields
springtime pendants
on every flower

faltering rhythm
the foal's legs
pencilling in dust

waiting for me to leave
sparrows sing
in the rear-view mirror

rising late
the swallow
finds new mud

hopping between branches
the chatter of robins

the sky turns red
each fire-season
a row of empty ATMs

teeth of the world

another sunny day
wasted
the lawn grins green

        hiding in the mailbox
        sunlight sinks
        into the snail's shell

another new year
still your shadow
has not faded

baby cricket
hops across the tiles
my chair creaks

spring downpour
clearing little bodies
from the gutters

rattling train –
lightning dries the sky
for just a second

teeth of the world

packing away
beach towels
the memory of sand

arriving home
just before the storm
a sweet wind

pine needles
become mammoth
the beetle pioneers

Second

teeth of the world

first waves –
I wade into the soft
conversation of morning

up and down the path
shadows
from unfinished clouds

after the birds
naught but
a garden of patches

fighting to recall
the little river's name –
a slow homecoming

the sky
is a loose sketch
plants exhale

in the windowsill
dead ants
ring the crumbs

teeth of the world

blue and white stripes
on the carpet
a bald moon shedding hair

ocean thumps the shore
each night
rust on the balcony

the tide races home
promises
stretch between us

uncertain palette
streaking down from the sky
I run for the washing

Christmas bloat –
another bag
of wrapping paper

crushed beneath
taxi after taxi –
elm leaves

the last feather
flutters between his teeth
pine trees creak

a chainsaw echoes
between trees
moss colonising stone

leaning into the wind
empty windows
on the old house

Ashley Capes

weather report –
an indrawn breath
from the whole town

birds at dawn
covering each sob
like a fossil

Garden Haiku

deflated –
cobwebs stretch
across my gloves

ants swarm the chasm
Godzilla with a shovel

new weeds
the chill of sunscreen
on my neck

Third

teeth of the world

skyscrapers –
teeth of the world
leave no bite-marks

tomorrow grows short
we jigsaw
the important things in

beneath our taxi's
paint job
rally car numbers

Ashley Capes

bunched together
in the dark
sleeping gondola

spread across the horizon
red pin pricks
on the highway

even crowds
in the postcard
have a better view

teeth of the world

in a rush –
prying our smiles
from the camera

in my yawning
the death rattle
of an alarm clock

more napalm
rolls from your tongue
the sky plays Holst

only wars, debts
and cars
seem to get handed down

supermarket
meat section
a lonely grape

fridge light
beaming from the black
dawn hesitates

teeth of the world

into the busker's song
a line about
my Pink Floyd shirt

pedestrians flow
almost one with the wall
the old beggar

outrunning joggers
a lunch bell
from across the park

chasing my nephew
across the yard
big bubbles

yet another test
putting picture books
into storage

whispering goodnight
to headlights on the wall

memories –
old wallpaper
quite unable to peel

right before dawn –
the pearlescence
of your breath

she runs across the sky
toes slick with morning

atop the Duomo
so little space
for all the graffiti

giggling teens
a Nurse Ratched look
from the next row

locust-thick –
scent of lollies
in the carwash

teeth of the world

shelter sheds –
little jimmy deans
take their first puffs

grass still yellow
but finally
no socks tonight

old cicada -
grinding itself
into an echo

our clothesline
taut in the wind
war yet to come

darkening grass –
a final chorus
from the crickets

Thanks for reading!

More haiku by Ashley:

*orion tips the saucepan
old stone*

www.ingramcontent.com/pod-product-compliance
Lightning Source LLC
Chambersburg PA
CBHW030530010526
44110CB00048B/1070